THE STORY OF HIP-HOP

Melanie J. Cornish

Copyright © ticktock Entertainment Ltd 2009

First published in Great Britain in 2009 by ticktock Media Ltd,
The Old Sawmill, 103 Goods Station Road, Tunbridge Wells, Kent, TN1 2DP

project editor and picture researcher: Ruth Owen
ticktock project designer: Simon Fenn

Thank you to Lorraine Petersen and the members of nasen

ISBN 978 1 84696 946 1 pbk

Printed in China

Picture credits (t=top; b=bottom; c=centre; l=left; r=right):
AFP/Getty Images: 29. Jerry Arcieri/Corbis: 12-13. Corbis: 21. David Corio: 6b, 16, 17, 18b, 22. diverseimages/Getty
Images: 26. Film Magic/Getty Images: 19tl, 23. Getty Images: 7, 8, 19b, 20, 27. Clayton Hauck: 28.
Chi Modu/diverseimages.net: 18t, 19cr, 24. Peter Morgan/Reuters/Corbis: 25. Michael Ochs Archive/Getty Images: 9.
Ernest Paniccioli: 6t. Monifa Perry: 11. Shutterstock: OFC, 1, 2-3, 4-5, 14-15, 18-19 (background), 24-25 (background), 31.

Every effort has been made to trace copyright holders, and we apologise in advance for any omissions. We would be
pleased to insert the appropriate acknowledgments in any subsequent edition of this publication.

CONTENTS

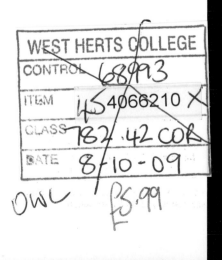

CHAPTER 1 | WHERE IT ALL BEGAN

Hip-Hop was born in the early 1970s. It began on the streets of the South Bronx, in New York City.

Since then, Hip-Hop culture has brought people together from all over the world. They celebrate Hip-Hop's four basic elements – emceeing, DJing, break-dancing and graffiti art.

Hip-Hop began as a street corner culture. Today, it is a worldwide, billion-dollar industry.

Most people agree that the "Forefather" of Hip-Hop is Kool Herc.

Kool Herc is a DJ in New York. In the early 1970s, he started to hold block parties in his neighbourhood.

DJ Kool Herc

Hundreds of local kids and adults went to Kool Herc's parties. They enjoyed the music played by DJs such as Kool Herc and Grandmaster Flash.

In 1973, DJ Kool Herc's sister, Cindy Campbell, had a house party. The party was at 1520 Sedgwick Avenue.

It is said to be the first Hip-Hop party ever held.

Grandmaster Flash

The party put 1520 Sedgwick Avenue on the map as the birthplace of Hip-Hop.

1520 SEDGWICK AVE.

CHAPTER 2

WHAT IS HIP-HOP?

Hip-Hop is made up of four basic elements.

EMCEEING

An MC is an artist who writes rhymes or poems. Then, he or she raps (says) them over a beat.

Emceeing began in Africa. African poets delivered their folk tales over drums and other instruments.

Rakim was the first MC to use internal rhyming. This means he uses more patterns than normal within the bars of a song.

In 1979, the Sugarhill Gang released the single *Rapper's Delight*. It was the first "Gold" selling record in Hip-Hop. It sold over 500,000 copies.

Rapper's Delight was even heard in countries that had no idea what Hip-Hop was!

The song was a big hit around the world and...

...people wanted to hear more.

Wonder Mike   Master Gee   Big Bank Hank

" Sugarhill Gang made dreams come true for those of us who couldn't sing or dance. "

MC Ice Cube

DJING

The DJ gives the MC a musical background against which to perform his or her poetry.

Hip-Hop DJs learned to make different sounds using the needles on their turntables.

DJs such as Grandmaster Flash, Caz and Grand Wizard Theodore invented scratching.

Scratching is when a DJ plays a very short part of a song backwards and forwards. They do this by moving the record using their hand.

New York based DJ Scratch is famous for his scratching techniques.

" I still get excited when I hear my music on the radio today, and it's been over 20 years since I started. "

DJ Scratch

DJ Scratch

B-BOYS AND B-GIRLS

As Hip-Hop music spread through the streets, parks and schools of America, a new style of dancing developed. It was called "break-dancing".

B-Boys and B-Girls developed their dances alongside the Hip-Hop MCs and DJs.

Break-dancers were often part of
groups called "crews".

Crews would have dancing "battles".
The crowd would decide who was
the best crew.

The final element of Hip-Hop culture is graffiti art.

New York City became a centre for graffiti art at the same time as Hip-Hop was really getting going.

Graffiti became linked with Hip-Hop. Graffiti artists would often practise their tags and create art in places where DJs and MCs were making music.

Like emceeing and break-dancing, graffiti was a way for people to express themselves.

CHAPTER 3

THE GOLDEN YEARS

For many Hip-Hop fans the mid 1980s to mid 1990s are the most important time in Hip-Hop history.

In 1984, Run-DMC from New York, was the first Hip-Hop act to receive a Grammy nomination.

Daryl (DMC) McDaniels

Jason (Jam Master Jay) Mizell

Their first album *Run-D.M.C.* went Gold. It sold just over 650,000 copies. The album featured the track *It's Like That*.

In 1986, Run-DMC's *Raising Hell* album went three times "Platinum". This album sold over three million copies.

In 2002, Run-DMC announced their retirement.

Joseph (The Reverend Run) Simmons

In the late 1980s, Hip-Hop artists such as Queen Latifah, Salt-N-Pepa, Public Enemy, A Tribe Called Quest and Big Daddy Kane began making records.

Queen Latifah is now a successful movie actress.

All these artists have been recognised by VH1's *Hip-Hop Honors* show for their contribution to Hip-Hop.

Big Daddy Kane started Hip-Hop fashion trends. He wore sweat suits and lots of gold jewellery.

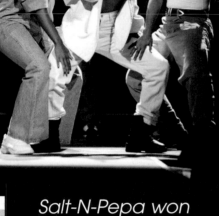

Salt-N-Pepa won
five Grammy awards.

A Tribe Called
Quest's lyrics
were positive.
Their message was
"just be yourself".

Public Enemy's political lyrics
talked about issues affecting
African-American people.

In 1986, one of the most controversial groups in Hip-Hop history emerged. They were called N.W.A.

N.W.A's lyrics talked about gang culture.
Kids were attracted to gangs because
they created their own rules.

But life in a gang could be violent and lead
to a life of crime.

Los Angeles police round up suspected gang members.

N.W.A also talked about how badly some police
officers treated young black and Hispanic men.

N.W.A's sound became known as "gangsta rap."

Many people felt N.W.A's lyrics encouraged violence against the police. Their lyrics also contained lots of swearing.

Some radio shows banned their music.
Their records had to carry a warning to parents.

However, N.W.A's music talked about the issues facing thousands of young men in inner cities, such as Los Angeles.

CHAPTER 4

THE LOST ONES

The 1990s saw the rise of two of Hip-Hop's most promising talents, The Notorious B.I.G and Tupac Shakur.

Biggie, as he was usually called, was born and brought up on the east coast of America in Brooklyn, New York.

He was signed to Sean "Diddy" Combs' Bad Boy Records.

Tupac was born in Harlem, New York.
He moved to Marin City, California, on the west coast, with his family in the early 1980s.

Tupac was signed to Death Row Records. This label was founded by Suge Knight and Dr. Dre.

Tupac (left) with Suge Knight

Both MCs were famous for their emceeing skills.

Their storytelling and unique delivery sold millions of records worldwide.

CHAPTER 5 MONEY AND SUCCESS

In the late 1990s, Hip-Hop artists such as Dr. Dre, Timbaland and Sean "Diddy" Combs were becoming rich and successful as producers.

They were in demand to create hit records and videos.

Dr. Dre in the studio with Snoop Dogg.

The 1990s saw many new stars emerge. Some, such as Jay Z, Busta Rhymes and Nas, are still making and selling albums today.

Hip-Hop records were selling millions of copies worldwide. Hip-Hop was big business!

Jay Z and Beyoncé are the ultimate
music industry "power couple".
They earned over £100 million in 2007.

CHAPTER 6

HIP-HOP TODAY

Today, Hip-Hop music and culture is bigger than ever.

Rappers can promote and sell their music on the internet without the backing of a record label.

The Cool Kids from America promoted their music through their page on *MySpace.com*.

Their success online got them a record deal.

Antoine (Mikey Rocks) Reed (top) and Evan (Chuck Inglish) Ingersoll

Some MCs are more than just musical superstars.
They have become very rich businessmen.

Sean "Diddy" Combs has businesses in the music
industry. He also owns restaurants, and has
produced designer ranges of clothes, shoes and
even wheels!

NEED TO KNOW WORDS

block party An informal, outdoor party where people from a neighbourhood come together and dance while a DJ plays music.

contribution The part someone plays in making something happen.

controversial Something that people disagree about.

culture A way of life, or a set of beliefs or shared interests and values that bring a group of people together.

DJing Playing records or CDs for an audience and using different techniques to make them sound great.

element A part of something.

emceeing Rapping (saying) words over a musical background.

emerge To come into being.

feud A long-running argument between two people or groups.

gangsta rap A type of Hip-Hop music that talked about the issues facing kids in inner cities.

Gold When a record has sales of over 500,000 in the USA and over 100,000 in the UK.

graffiti Colourful words and artworks created using spray paint cans.

Grammy An award given by the "National Academy of Recording Arts and Sciences" for an outstanding contribution within the music industry.

Hispanic People that come from Spanish-speaking countries in Central and South America, such as Mexico.

label A record company.

MC This is short for "Master of Ceremonies". MCs are people who host a show and introduce acts. In the Hip-Hop world, an MC is another name for a rapper.

nomination To be one of the people put forward for an award.

Platinum When a record has sales of over one million in the USA and over 300,000 in the UK.

producer A person who works with music artists in a recording studio to help them create their music.

promote To advertise something and make people aware of it.

tag When a graffiti artist marks something with their name.

unique The only one of its kind.

GET INTO HIP-HOP

If you are interested in getting into the Hip-Hop business here are some tips.

• Use websites such as *MySpace.com* to promote your music. Labels sometimes use these websites to find new artists.

• If you write your own lyrics, make sure you copyright your material. Copyrighting means you officially own the lyrics and no one else can use them without your permission. See: *http://www.copyrightservice.co.uk/*

• Apply for summer jobs at record labels and magazines. You might have to work for free, but these jobs can help you make good contacts. Check the law where you live to make sure you are old enough to take a job.

HIP-HOP ONLINE

Websites

http://www.DaveyD.com
The website of Hip-Hop journalist Davey D

http://www.rocksteadycrew.com/
The website of the world's most famous B-Boy crew

INDEX